AF479770

GOD MADE YOU

Serguina Rodriguez

Illustrated by Ira Baykovska

God made the sun.
God made the moon.

God made the Earth,
and God made YOU!

From every hair on your head,
to the tiny toes on your feet –

He made each part of you
so special and so sweet.

**The color of your eyes,
the shape of your nose –**

The smile on your face –
those are all things God chose!

See, He knew who you were
before you even had a name.

And He thought of all the great things
you could become one day!

Like, maybe a doctor? Or a teacher, or vet?
Maybe a scientist, or even President, better yet!

Whatever you become,
just know this is true –

God knows your heart,
and He loves you for you.

No matter where you live,
or the clothes that you wear...

No matter your favorite music,
or how you style your hair...

God knows His plans
to give you hope and a future.

You were made in His image
to love, forgive and nurture.

You're one of a kind,
because God set you apart.

He made you so precious,
unique, kind and smart.

The world needed someone
whose light always shines through.

And that's exactly what happened
when God made you.

About the Author

Serguina's passion for writing began when she was just a little girl who used to write letters to God. Her mother often reminds her of the times she would find pages of heartfelt messages, stories and poems in her bedroom, all dedicated to God, either writing to Him about her day or writing to the world about His unconditional love. This passion inspired her to subsequently earn a Bachelor's Degree in Broadcast Journalism from Suffolk University in Boston, MA, with which she was able to write and tell daily stories as a television news producer.

Now living back in her hometown in California, she is a wife and a mother of two little girls who are the sweetest, kindest souls. Since the moment she became a mother, she knew she would one day use her passion to write children's books centered around her strong Christian faith.

She hopes this book encourages parents to connect with their children and teach them about our awesome Creator, all while reminding them of how awesome they are and the endless possibilities of what they could become one day!

About
the Illustrator

Ira Baykovska is a children's book illustrator and a mom of two beautiful girls.

Ira has been drawing for as long as she can remember and sometimes cannot believe that this hobby has become her life-long career.

She has been working as a freelance illustrator since 2014 and has illustrated more than 20 books for kids. Ira has a degree in Graphic Design and currently lives and works in Lviv, Ukraine.

Visit Ira's website **www.baykovska.com**